A SHORT & EASY PRIMER ON THE ASSET MANAGEMENT INDUSTRY

The Bigger Picture: Learn How The Industry Works In Practice

WILLIAM J. FISHER

DEDICATION

This is for my family. They bring me joy
and the will to write.

CONTENTS

INTRODUCTION TO THE AUTHOR

Here's an immediate reveal: my true name is not William J. Fisher! It is a pen name I have adopted as I do not necessarily want to reveal my true self (just yet). There's nothing personal about it. I'm a professional who is currently working in the asset management industry. Having been here for many years, I will give you a view of how asset management is viewed from within the industry, not outside. I find it frustrating when books are written from 'experts' who are more academic in nature than practical. I find such books not accurately reflecting how the industry operates on a day-day basis.

When I first entered the industry years ago, I often found myself unable to grasp the fundamentals. The books I found were generic business books that applied to all of finance and not specific to asset management. Eventually I landed a role at one of the world's leading asset managers, and having now worked at the firm for many years and experienced changes in the industry first hand, I feel well positioned to write a book on asset management.

WHO IS THIS BOOK FOR?

For those who need a swift bird's eye view of the asset management industry!

While any numbers and dates I use in the book may be current, or old, depending on when you read this book, the themes and concepts covered in this book were relevant in the past, are relevant today, and will remain so going forward.

By reading this book, you will come out well versed to hold a mature conversation on what matters in the asset management industry. Perfect for if you are preparing for an interview, or if you just want an accessible yet thorough introduction into this field. It is also for working professionals who are already in the industry, possibly in a niche, or specialist role, and would like to get a better understanding of the bigger picture.

Think of this book as a primer, a crash-course, an 'essentials' book, a very short introduction to...

WHY IS THIS BOOK WORTH READING? WHAT'S IN IT FOR ME?

Don't we all wish we could quickly grab the low hanging fruits to become instantly smarter on a subject? The low hanging fruits give us enough confidence to tackle a subject. This book does exactly that.

The problem is that there aren't many books out there on the asset management industry. You're instead more likely to find books on fund management or portfolio management, and they tend to dive straight into portfolio construction, asset allocation, valuation and so on. Don't believe me? Have a quick browse on Amazon and you'll see what I mean. Very few actually explain the asset management business, the structure of the industry and how it is run at the corporate level. This is the problem I had when starting off. There was just too much opaqueness. With that in mind, I have written this short book for those who want a highly accessible, yet thorough look into the industry without getting too involved in valuation and jargon. Don't be fooled by the length of this book. Despite being short, it will give you an overview of the business in a manner that I've not seen other books give.

CHAPTER 1.
UNDERSTANDING THE
ASSET MANAGEMENT BUSINESS

What is the business all about?

Asset management is the process of managing money on behalf of clients. 'Managing' money means deploying your client's money in various types of investments (equities, debt or investments across both, which is known as multi-asset investments) in order to grow the pot size. The companies that offer such services are known as asset managers or investment managers. The practice itself can also be known as investment management. Global asset management is a huge business. The assets managed by all investment managers is close to $70 trillion at the time of writing. To put that into context, total financial assets worldwide is around $250 trillion. The number can vary depending on which source you use (some predict it to be closer to $300 trillion). People in the industry believe asset management makes up around a quarter of all financial assets worldwide.

How does an asset manager make money, and why would a client even want to give their money to be managed by an asset manager?

You can think of an asset manager as the 'middle-man' between the client and investments. The manager makes their money through commissions (the client pays what you call a management fee). Some relationships pay flat fees, while some managers can also get compensated based on how well a particular investment performs – this is called a performance fee.

So why would a client want to pay someone to manage their money. Why do they not do it themselves? Well think of it this way: Coca Cola is a company that specializes in making Coke. Apple specializes in making iPhones, iPads and other high-end electronics. The railway workers union in your country specializes in giving a voice to employees in the railway sector. What do they all have in common? Two things: they are all specialists in their own field, but they aren't specialists in taking money and investing it in order to grow it. That's why they will hire an investment manager to do the work for them.

Why would they need to invest? Well because they have employees who will one day retire and will need to be taken care of via a pension. The companies can either keep putting up their own cash to pay their retirees or they can try and grow a pot of money which becomes self-sustaining and can carry the weight. Which would you choose? The pressure of making constant cash contributions, or try and scale up by investing in the global markets?

Why hire an asset manager?

SITUATION	PROBLEM	SOLUTION
I am great at making soft drinks	But how do I grow my workforce's pension pots? I am running out of reserve cash	I'll hire an asset manager who will invest the money and grow it. I'll give them a fee

What is the role of asset management in the wider world? How does it contribute to society?

For you and I, the common man and woman, investing in products offered by asset managers is a nice way to invest in the markets without having to do the manual dirty work. We just give a fee and the rest of the work is done. Asset management offers people the chance to move their money out of cash and current bank accounts, which give very low interest rates, and deploy it to something useful.

On a larger scale, asset management is the facilitator of development in economies. With yield becoming ever more elusive, institutional clients are searching for ever more creative ways to generate returns. A way to do this has been by locking their money in ever longer-term investments that won't generate returns today but in the long run they will. What could those kinds of investments be? Well, consider infrastructure for example. Building bridges and railways takes time and money. Pension funds have the money (billions of dollars) and the ability to wait.

Building such infrastructure is directly beneficial to the development of the economy and asset managers give pension funds access to such investment opportunities.

Who are the industry's main players?

The world's largest asset manager is BlackRock, with over $6.5 trillion in assets under management (AUM) at the time of writing. Think about that for a second. That's $6,500,000,000,000 worth of client money that they manage. If BlackRock were a nation that figure would make them approximately the third-largest economy by GDP. It would be larger than Japan, Germany, and the UK. For the record, China is around $10T while the US is $18T or thereabouts. BlackRock has largely grown inorganically (meaning they grew through buying and merging with other companies. This is called mergers and acquisitions). The two big acquisitions were Merrill Lynch Investment Managers (MLIM) in 2006 and Barclays Global Investors (BGI) in 2009. The BGI acquisition happened after the 2008 financial crisis and propelled BlackRock straight to the top of the global asset manager rankings. With the BGI acquisition also came iShares, which is a market leading ETF business and a key component of BlackRock's business today.

Hot behind BlackRock's heels is Vanguard with around $5 trillion in AUM. Vanguard is hugely popular brand in its home market, the US. Vanguard is known as the industry's leading 'low-cost' provider. Think of them as your provider of cheap goods – the budget, low-cost provider. They have done particularly well on the back of the financial crisis with clients demanding lower-fee products.

Some other legendary names in asset management include State Street Global Advisors (SSgA), Allianz Global Investors (AGI), PIMCO and JP Morgan Asset Management (JPMAM). Each have their specialism. SSgA were the inventors of the hugely popular ETFs. PIMCO have a reputation as a leading fixed income house while JPMAM have their reputation in active management.

An insider's view: how people in asset management think about the business itself.

The best way to understand asset management is to understand it from the perspective of people working in the industry. Now, this isn't so simple. What's tricky is that it is difficult to get a holistic picture of the entire industry. There just isn't data out there, or an aggregator that can simplify things. What people in the industry tend to do is to focus on their specialist area and try and bring transparency to that space. Having worked in a role that required me to think about the whole of market, I have developed a picture over the years and it is aligned with how people across the different areas of asset management think about their business. Here is the secret sauce: broadly speaking, asset management can be thought of as a three-dimensional space: asset class, client type and geography. It's a lot more complex than that, of-course, but it's a simple and concise way of thinking about the industry. Let's go through each of these dimensions.

Asset class
These are the 'investments' an asset manager can make to grow the pot of money once the client hands over the money to them. They can invest in equity funds, fixed income funds, multi-asset funds, alternatives funds, cash (money market funds) and so on.

Client type
These are the different types of investors out there. They can broadly be thought of as retail investors, or institutional investors. Retail investors are the common man or woman on the street, both you and I. Institutional investors are corporations e.g. pension funds, insurers, financial corporates, official institutions (sovereign wealth funds) and so on. Individual investors pool their money with other individuals (through a collective investment scheme such as a mutual fund) so that the size of the pot is

big enough to create scale. Institutional investors can have their own separate account as the money they have on hand to give to asset managers is a lot bigger.

Geography

Geography can refer to two things: the client domicile view or the product domicile view, and is a source of much confusion within the industry. Let me explain what each means. The client domicile view explains where the money is coming from. For example, let's say an asset manager sets up a $30 million portfolio (a collection of investments) for their client and it is entirely investing in US stocks such as McDonalds, Apple, Ford, Verizon and so on. The clients, however, may be based in Germany (e.g. a set of wealthy German investors who want exposure to US stocks). Using this example, the client domicile view would say there is $30 million of assets under management in Germany, whereas the product domicile view would say there is $30 million in US stocks. Get it? There's a small difference but it is a difference non-the-less. The point of all this is that it creates much confusion among people. Should the money be attributed to the US, or to Germany? Of course, each country would like to claim ownership of the assets to show their market is big, and with opportunities.

CHAPTER 2.
WHAT PEOPLE IN THE INDUSTRY DISCUSS AND DEBATE

The battle between passive and active investing. Which investing style rules?

Know one thing. There's two big investing styles in asset management. Active investing, and passive investing, also known as index investing.

Both use a benchmark with which to compare against. This can be the local stock market, for example, such as the S&P 500. The benchmark reflects the general state of the market. Think of it as an 'average state'. The difference between active and index investing is in what they want to achieve.

Active investing is all about trying to beat the returns of the benchmark while passive investing is all about trying to match the market. So of course, it's a no-brainer that an investor would choose active investing in order to get better returns than the benchmark, instead of just trying to match it, correct? Well no, not entirely correct. Studies have shown that over the long-run, the steady tortoise beats the hare. Anyone that has tried trading will be able to relate. You can get excited after making a few gains, but once you try and up the risk, it's pretty easy to lose your money. Slow and steady sometimes does the trick.

A couple of decades ago, people bought into the idea of passive investing (just trying to match the market) and went as far as creating a type of investment vehicle called the exchange traded fund (ETF). What do ETFs do? Well, they invest in every company in the S&P 500 (our example) so that the portfolio looks exactly like the S&P 500 index. Here, the S&P 500 is the market because it spans a large section of the economy.

ETFs rapidly shot up in popularity. They allowed the investor to get access to the index that they were tracking in one shot. The ETF would invest in the various companies in the index so that if you bought just one unit of the ETF you would have exposure to the whole market. What a neat trick. ETFs now make up $3 trillion in assets under management and are one of the fastest growing areas in asset management. Index tracking products outside the ETF world are also high in demand.

So since index investing is fast rising in popularity, will active investing just die out?

Having read what I wrote above, some of you must be thinking index investing is more preferable to active investing. After all, the fact that over the long-run, index investing generally beats active investing in terms of returns, must surely mean the active managers are not up to the job? Also incorrect. There will always be a handful of star portfolio managers out there who are consistently beating the market. They do exist. Just that they are a rare breed.

And also remember, it is hard-wired in human psychology to want more. We are never satisfied with the status quo. With each passing generation, there will always be some among us who think they will be able to beat the market. So no, the death of active investing is not going to happen. Some will succeed!

To put things into perspective, traditional active products are indeed getting squeezed out, but in return, other specialist areas, such as infrastructure, are gaining in popularity. Active equities (the traditional group) has had a troublesome few years after the 2008 financial crisis, with investors pulling out bucket loads of money from funds focused on actively navigating company stocks. With profits hard to come by, traditionally popular stocks have had a hard time generating profits, and with this active equity funds have also found it hard to generate profits. But it would be foolish to completely disregard investing in stocks. Could you imagine them being excluded from a multi-asset portfolio? No, you couldn't because stock picking is a traditionally popular business.

In fact, Robert Pozen and Theresa Hamacher of Harvard University and Nicsa, respectively, wrote an article in 2015 challenging the concept of why the active vs passive debate is binary at all. Why should it be one or the other? Why could it not be both? Active managers actually help to make the markets more efficient by buying underpriced securities and selling overpriced securities. That's the whole point of being an active manager: you look for pricing mismatches and exploit them. This very act helps prices to go back to their natural equilibrium where supply equals demand. Index investing makes markets inefficient because index funds change holdings not according to company fundamentals but according to inflows and outflows of money. This in turn creates opportunity for active managers to 'outperform' the market once again because they'll be able to identify these mispriced securities. And so the wheel keeps moving: active investing leads to efficiency which helps index investing. Index investing leads to inefficiencies which then presents opportunities for active managers to show their worth.

As you can see, it's like nature's ecosystem where every species has a role to play in balancing the food chain. Active and index investing work hand-in-hand.

Active and index investing work in cycles. One will not defeat the other.

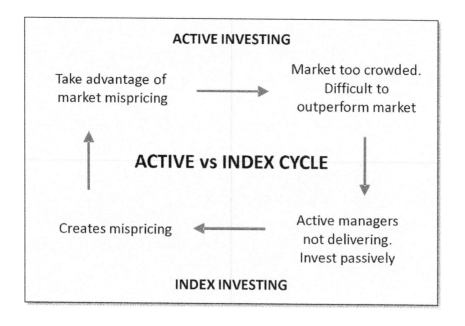

Shareholder interest can diverge from management focus.

You've already guessed that this will be a sensitive topic. If you really want to understand the mind of a business leader in asset management then this section will give you a massive head start.

The first thing to understand is that shareholders (the people who own the company) have a set of wishes. The second thing to understand is that management (the people who are employed to run the business) also have a set of wishes. The final point to understand is that they will not always align with each other.

I'll share with you a common conflict. I've seen it over and over again while working in the industry. It's actually not limited to asset management. This sort of conflict of interest can happen in any industry. Here goes...

Shareholders will want to explore how they can capture not just the market they are playing in, but also new areas that are yet to be tapped. This, however, puts pressure on management who may argue that these new avenues are just not accessible and so they shouldn't be judged on whether they have been able to capture market share in these new areas.

Shareholders want to see their company as the best
in the business. Their company may only be
focused on a particular segment of the US retail
market, for example, but they may be keen to look
at their company versus the whole US retail market
instead of just that section that they are playing in.
Let's suppose half of the retail market is closed
because that portion of the market is monopolized
by another player. Clearly there's no assets to gain
because there just will not be any sales
opportunities according to management. The
shareholders, however, will say that over the long
run, everything is flexible. There's a conflict here.

Management also look good if they have a big
market share so it's not always in their interests to
'grow' the pie otherwise their share will look worse.
On the other hand, astute managers may recognize
that their market share is already flat lining and
difficult to grow further. In such cases it is difficult
to justify asking for more resource (money) because
there may be a belief that the unit isn't going to be
able to do anything more. In such cases,
management may want to 'grow' the pie to show
there is 'opportunity'. It's all a balancing act at the
end of the day.

Such a phenomenon has a name: the total market view versus the addressability view.

Total market is used to describe the market in totality. For example, one could say the total retail market consists of both the addressable portion (the portion that independent asset managers can try and capture) and the non-addressable 'captive' portion. This captive portion can't be won over because it's likely assets that are being fed to an asset manager if the parent is a powerful bank. Here, the bank will have lots of retail clients and they'll just refer any money that clients want to invest to their asset management arm. It's a totally closed distribution unit. Independent managers outside the unit will have no chance of getting the assets so they'll prefer to not include the assets as part of their market share sizing exercise. Shareholders, however, will not be so keen to ignore that portion. 'What can we do to tap into that market?'

Mutual funds versus retail: what's the difference?

This is also another source of much confusion. The terms are used interchangeably but aren't the same thing. The story behind this is that mutual funds are a collection of people's money. The fund then invests in various asset classes. Usually, it's used to describe the cumulative money collected from retail investors (the average person on the street). So people will say 'mutual fund assets' interchangeably with 'retail assets'. The reality is that this is inaccurate.

Mutual funds actually have share classes. These are like your economy class and your business class on an airline. You can own a share of the fund and you can own it as a retail investor or an institutional investor. Institutional share classes have higher minimum investment thresholds – think of them as business class.

So to try and use mutual funds to describe retail isn't entirely accurate. You're going to be including a portion of institutional money in there. The problem starts when you try and do an overall market sizing by including institutional into the mix. You have retail represented by mutual funds, but you'll have a bit of double counting in institutional because it's represented in both institutional data and a bit of mutual fund data. You'll end up over-sizing the asset management universe. So that $70 trillion industry size is very possibly slightly oversized!

☐

Being precise versus being ball park.

Being too precise can actually be a drawback in the world of asset management. Surprised? Well, the reason why is because it takes skill to be both a high level generalist of the industry and a bottoms-up specialist who has every detail under their belt.

When you end up working with senior business leaders, they're not always so concerned with detail to the decimal point. They're more focused on the bigger picture and what direction the ship should be heading in. On the other hand, if you work with a mid-level manager, their performance is more likely to be judged on level of accuracy. After all, accuracy is a quick way to gain respect and trust.

So the challenge starts here. Just how easy is it to be both that high-level bird who can fly across all the major themes and that analyst who knows every detail? The answer is, not easy at all. Being immersed in the detail is a full-time task and it takes tremendous effort to then fly back to a high level.

The solution is usually to have two employees or two teams if the task is substantial. One team will focus on the detail while the other focuses on the bigger picture. Imagine if you are able to do both. You instantly become unique to your team.

CHAPTER 3.
THE DATA SYSTEMS USED BY THE INDUSTY

This chapter is especially useful for those interviewing for a new role. It will give you a head start in being able to demonstrate you have a level of understanding about the day-to-day systems being used. Once again, I must stress this book is not about portfolio management so we are not looking at portfolio management systems. I will leave that to the great portfolio management books out there.

Let's start off by using the client type model we previously touched upon. We will discuss the systems used by people in both the retail world and the institutional world to track momentum in the industry. The bottom line is this: data coverage in the retail market is great. Data in the institutional space, however, is very limited. After all, why would institutional clients be willing to disclose data on huge portfolios worth billions of Dollars?

In the retail space, there are many data providers and each has a unique selling point. The more nimble asset management teams will try to utilize the best parts of each.

Broadridge is one of the more popular data vendors. They collect fund data from the entire market. A direct competitor is Morningstar, who are also well known throughout the industry. The difference is that Morningstar provide performance data as well. This is information on what your portfolio's returns were (very frequently the performance is compared to against the benchmark index). You then have Simfund, which covers the same data but aggregates the best of both Broadridge and Morningstar and also adds its own refinement on top. Broadridge has an extensive classification system for the asset classes, broken down into sector and geography. So for example, you could have 'UK equities', or 'Global high yield fixed income'. Morningstar and Simfund have the advantage of performance data so that you can compare fund performance, which Broadridge does not provide at the time of writing.

The problem with retail data is that full coverage on just how much money (called flows) pulled in each month comes with a time lag. This poses a problem, especially for people on the job that need data as soon as possible. The trends you see in the data may have evolved or changed by the time the data is ready to use, so you would always be talking in the past tense.

There is a partial solution to this: enter EPFR Global. EPFR have been around a long time, evolving from providing information on emerging markets, to becoming more of a holistic mutual fund and ETF data provider like a Simfund or a Broadridge. They try to fix the problem of timeliness by providing data updates on both a daily, weekly and monthly basis. The daily or weekly datasets can be used to get a much faster sense of which funds are pulling in the money, which asset classes have done well and which managers are the most compelling. The flip-side of the coin is that data coverage can be patchier than on Broadridge. Not all asset managers report to the daily and weekly data. It is therefore best to think of EPFR as more of a directional indicator of markets than a source for absolute flow numbers.

In the institutional space... well, there's not many comprehensive data providers out there.

You should just learn to accept it. There aren't many comprehensive data sources out there. The reason for this is because institutional money is serious business. Not all institutions investing will want to reveal what their holdings are, so it is difficult to get much information. And it's not surprising at all. A data vendor called eVestment Alliance has made an attempt at covering the global institutional space but data is self-reported by managers and can be inconsistent at times. There really isn't much else out there. You have industry reports covering specific areas in the institutional space, such as the Sovereign Wealth Fund Institute's (SWFI) report on SWFs around the globe. There is also an online database service by Spence Johnson called iMiM which looks to cover the European institutional asset management space and give it much more accessibility like in the retail space. It's still work in progress at the time of writing so eVestment continues to be the data source of choice for many. Finally, you have popular websites such as Pensions & Investments (P&I) and Investments Pensions Europe (IPE) that have become the go-to source for pensions news (which make up a large portion of institutional assets). However, as you dig further, you'll see there's just no source out there that aggregates everything into one place. So if your manager asks you to build a picture of the institutional world, just know that you are undertaking a massive task!

CHAPTER 4.
THE BIG TRENDS SHAPING THE ASSET MANAGEMENT LANDSCAPE

Thinking about macro and micro factors is a good way to analyze any industry, including asset management.

A good way of thinking about the trends that may shape an industry is to think about the macro and micro factors in play.

Macro factors
Macro factors are industry-wide trends that can impact any company in that industry. These trends aren't necessarily under the control of the company. The following factors impact any industry, including asset management: demographic factors, economic factors, natural factors, technological factors, political factors, cultural factors and regulation. This is what I refer to as DENTPCR. Not all of them apply to the industry in question, but you can simply go through the list and tick the ones that are relevant.

Micro factors

Micro factors are factors that are under the control of a company to an extent. They include relationships with intermediaries and customers, and relationship of the company with itself (i.e. how it is run).

Use the Porters 5 forces model to bring the analysis together

A good way of analyzing these factors is through the Porter's 5 Forces model.

The Porter's Five Forces model helps you to understand how to analyze an industry.

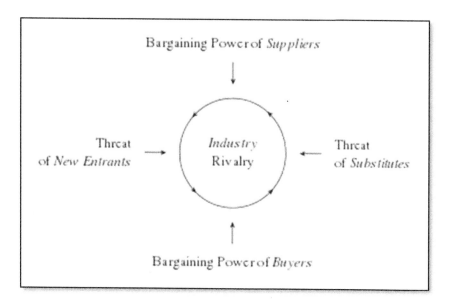

Source: Wikipedia

You can also use this model for interviews, strategic thinking, and problem solving.

The beauty of this model is that it can be used to answer so many things. For those interviewing for jobs, if you are asked what are the most important factors to consider before starting a business, you can also apply this model. It's flexible!

And by the way, if you would like to know more about this tool, and generally how to think systematically and strategically, then watch out for what will be my future book on strategic thinking. Of-course, that depends on whether I get the sales for this book.

So what are the key trends driving asset management I hear you say?

The key macro factors impacting asset management are demographic, economic, technological and regulation. Out of these three, I would argue technology and regulation are the biggest ones to watch out for. The key micro factor is competition. I'll explain in more detail below.

Demographics: the increasing lifespan of humans has a direct impact!

When it comes to demographics, think no further than the increasing lifespans of humans. The way it works is linked to the Coca-Cola example we used at the beginning of this book. Once again, Coca-Cola are a company that specializes in making Coke. They don't specialize in looking after their employees after they retire. However, the reality is that their employees will retire one day and will need to be looked after until they pass away. Coca-Cola will have started a pension pot for their employees.

The pension pot in the past would have been called a defined benefit pension (DB) but lately a lot of new pension schemes are opened as defined contribution schemes (DC). I won't get into what the differences are but just know that with DB schemes the responsibility is with Coca-Cola to make sure their employees have enough of a big pot for when they retire, while with DC the responsibility rests with the worker to sort themselves out by choosing which asset classes to invest in (are they even qualified to do this? Is that fair?).

So anyway, let's say Coca-Cola opened up a DB scheme for their employees at some point in the past. They will calculate the annual payment they will need to make to each employee once they retire. The challenge with this is figuring out how many years to pay for. You just don't know how long they will live for. Of course, there are studies out there giving an indication of average life span and so on, but the reality is that people are living longer than ever before. Technology and advances in living standards mean we can now all live longer after retiring.

So the way Coca-Cola can try and resolve this is by giving an asset manager the responsibility to grow the pension pot ('the assets'). And it need not be just one asset manager. They can ask asset managers to fight for the opportunity to manage a slice of the pie. The winner will add that to their 'assets under management'. So that's where 'assets under management comes from'. It's just a reflection of how much of client money a manager is looking after.

The longer people are living, the more pressure it adds to everyone involved in the value chain to generate decent returns. Traditional safe investments, such as investing in government bonds just will not cut it. And since interest rates have plummeted since the financial crisis in 2008, asset managers are being forced to be more creative with their investment selections. They are being forced to venture further out into the risk spectrum and invest in more exotic investments. How about some infrastructure? Or even investing in paintings? You get the picture.

To everyone looking to get into the industry, pay attention! The traditional way of investing in the world of asset management is changing fast, and new traditional are emerging.

Economic conditions: current economic conditions are making it harder for managers to grow their clients' money
The gap between how much the size of the pension pot is (the assets) and how much Coca-Cola thinks it will need to pay retirees (the liabilities) is called the funding gap. Funding gaps are getting bigger across the world. With the onset of the financial crisis in 2008, growing assets has also been much harder against the backdrop of highly uncertain market conditions.

We are now in a world of near-zero or negative interest rates and this is having a big impact on the type of asset classes that are in demand. As explained just now, clients are wanting to move out of lower yielding asset classes and into higher yielding asset classes because it's getting more and more difficult to generate returns in tough market conditions.

A good way to think about this is by asking what asset classes are impacted by movements in interest rates? Well, bonds (or fixed income) is the key one! What's happened is that clients are moving out of government bonds (bonds that the government issued) because interest rates are very low. You're getting very little return. They're moving to more risky asset classes, desperate for returns (to match funding gaps, for example). Riskier asset classes include specialist areas such as alternatives (hedge funds, real estate, infrastructure, private equity) and multi-asset portfolios that combine a variety of different asset classes. You're also seeing a new breed of funds that are tackling market conditions, called minimum volatility funds. The fund (read: portfolio) will choose securities that are resistant to economic swings and roundabouts during difficult market conditions.

There's of course other economic trends in place but you get the picture. Any major event will feed its way into the asset management market. For example, consider oil prices, which have been on a massive downward trend. Sovereign wealth funds in the Middle East have been pulling out money from their 'fund' accounts with asset managers so that they can use the money to stabilize their economy. Remember, oil is a key source of revenue for oil rich countries. If oil prices are suffering then these nations will have less revenues with which to run their economy. So where shall they look? Well, look no further than the bloated Sovereign Wealth Funds which are in the hundreds of billions of dollars in terms of assets. These Sovereign Wealth Funds are essentially reserve funds for these nations. For asset managers, however, it isn't great news. How can it be good news if your client is pulling money out from the pot? It means the assets you manage is lower, and you'll also therefore be earning less commission on average.

Technology: is the big enabler. The game changer that will allow asset managers to move into a new era. The factor that will allow asset managers to get closer to the man on the street There's a reason why you haven't heard of some of the big companies in asset management, or in investment banking as a matter of fact. Before the financial crisis, many hadn't even heard of prominent banking players such as Goldman Sachs. These players traditionally focused on business with large companies, and not the man or woman on the street (the retail investor). The financial crisis changed all that and Goldman Sachs is now a household name, whether for the right or wrong reasons.

All this is anecdotal to the effect technology is having on asset management. Big data is not just an asset management phenomenon. With the rise of the internet, mobile and smart technology, it's easier than ever before to capture people's tastes, thoughts and decision making. Companies are seeing the opportunity to data mine and identify patterns in people's behaviors. In theory, this should help them with decision making. In reality, asset managers are still trying to figure out exactly how to put things into practice. There's just so many sources out there. One could look at Twitter, Facebook, coffee shops, posh restaurants, the list goes on. Imagine being able to get hold of data providing insight into how much employment there is in the economy. You could use that data to get a gauge for job creation in the industry before official data comes out! That's the power of big data. With this data, you can get a feel of whether stocks in that country are likely to perform well. Sounds like a good investment idea!

One thing to bear in mind though is that asset managers have been slow adopters in this space. Naturally, technology companies such as Facebook and Google collect data as part of their bread and butter. That makes them a threat to asset management firms! Imagine that. Could you see Facebook entering asset management? Seems absurd right now but people within the industry see them as a real threat.

Another massive story is the rise of robo-advisory. Robo-advisors, such as Betterment in the US, and Nutmeg in the UK are online robots (algorithms) that help to create an investment portfolio. Their advantages are that they allow the common person to consolidate their various financial accounts into one place. What's the benefit of that? Well, it's always a lot easier to manage things in one place. You'll usually get a 'fun' questionnaire asking you about your attitudes to investing. How much of a risk taker are you? Do you like equities or fixed income? If you lost your savings how much would that impact you, and so on? Based on that, you'll get a risky or conservative portfolio recommended to you by the robot so that you don't need to go and figure it out yourself. It takes the hassle out of investing and is like having your own financial adviser but at a much cheaper cost. The one thing to bear in mind is that it's a fairly new phenomenon and hasn't yet been tested on whether it can help you and I to manage our money in all kinds of market conditions, good and bad.

Regulation: is affecting all regions all the time
In the US we have the DOL fiduciary rule. In Europe we have Mifid II. Both look to essentially hand more power to the customer. If you observed closely, you'll remember bargaining power of customers was one of the factors in the Porter's 5

Forces model which explains the competitive dynamics in an industry. At the time of writing, the DOL rule went under review following Donald Trump's election as US president. That put a lot of US policies under review. As for Mifid II, well the UK and Netherlands were the first two to implement a version of its rules in their local markets respectively. The result was an increase in use of passive funds (as opposed to active). Essentially what Mifid II suggests is that customers need to be charged in a more transparent manner. Many asset managers sell their products not directly to the investor but through an intermediary such as a financial advisor. The financial advisor will then recommend that product to the investor. In return for recommending the product, the asset manager will pass on some of the fees collected from the investor onto the financial advisor. This practice has historically led to all sorts of behavior, such as some financial advisor firms recommending more expensive products so that the fee they collect, called a 'rebate' is higher. An embedded bias towards higher fee active products. Now if this sort of rebate is banned then some think it makes the financial advisor more neutral and they would be indifferent towards recommending a low cost and an expensive solution, focusing more on the merit of the product. That's exactly what Mifid II aimed to do.

Competition: it's a two-horse race and prices are going down!
There's two asset managers dominating the world of asset management. The first is Vanguard, who as we explained earlier are big on low fees. The other is BlackRock, the world's largest and most diversified manager. Vanguard have been getting closer to BlackRock in recent years and some predict they will surpass BlackRock one day. BlackRock have responded to Vanguard's low fee strategy by launching their own suite of low fee products. The biggest example of this is in the ETF world where prices keep falling. The amount of assets Vanguard and BlackRock are raising from clients is so far ahead of competition that the competition isn't to be seen in the distant horizon.

Some active managers are not as threatened by Vanguard's low fee strategy. They see active management as on a different pricing point and not entirely in competition with passive. They do not feel the pressure to lower fees, and that's really a reflection of the way the industry is headed in. When it comes to passive offerings, such as ETFs, pricing matters. At the other end of the spectrum, you have asset managers delivering better returns than the market through a lot of skill, judgment and expert analysis on the markets. They are not as concerned by pricing pressure as they believe their value-add is worth the fee.

The general fee compression trend is structural, however. Investors have become more sophisticated and know where to look for value add so prices will continue to go down over time.

CHAPTER 5.
WHAT WILL ASSET MANAGEMENT LOOK LIKE 10 YEARS FROM NOW?

The barbell will continue to intensify.

Looking at current growth rates, global asset management will probably grow to around $90T-$100T from the $70 trillion in investable assets today. In the previous chapter we discussed some of the big trends impacting asset managers, both micro and macro. These factors will push investors into either side of the investment spectrum – the one side being active investing, and the other side passive investing.

This means we are going to see the barbell continue to intensify. To picture this, imagine a barbell with bulky weights on either side, but a slim middle. You can also think of an hourglass to picture this. The industry has been moving in this direction for many years. Passive investing stands on one side while active investing sits on the other side. Both sides continue to bulk up while the middle (which is traditional active) gets squeezed out.

The barbell explains the direction of travel in asset management.

Source: Credit Suisse

In the middle were traditional actively managed categories. Now, some investors are moving to low-cost passive strategies (such as ETFs) while others are moving further up the risk ladder to invest in more illiquid strategies such as real estate or infrastructure which offer higher returns.

We will see asset managers merging and consolidating.

We're also likely to see consolidation in the industry. The industry has evolved in a way in which specialist managers were allowed to thrive. They would focus on a specialist area, such as emerging markets, and would not do anything else. This worked for many years but after the financial crisis, ever more volatile market swings made it imperative for asset managers to have a wide range of capabilities so that if one business unit suffers then the other unit can hold up well. A good example of this is BlackRock, the world's largest asset manager. They have a presence in all major asset classes (equities, fixed income, multi-asset, alternatives). They have also been quick to jump on the bandwagon of key themes that are currently in demand (technology, socially responsible investments). Such a company is likely to be able to weather the storms gone by and new ones yet to come. The ones that do not diversify their business will suffer and all it will take is one bad run in their focus area and the business is wiped out. As a result, we will likely see some of the specialist asset managers being bought out by larger managers who are looking to bulk up their capabilities by making 'bolt-on' acquisitions. In Europe, we have already seen examples of this in 2016 and 2017. French powerhouse Amundi acquired Italian manager Pioneer to help boost its presence in Italy – one of the leading retail markets in Europe. UK managers Standard Life and Aberdeen announced a merger in 2017 to create the UK's largest asset manager and one of the top players in Europe by assets under management. Both Standard Life and Aberdeen have suffered withdrawal of money from clients in recent years due to volatile market conditions and struggling fund performance.

A number of managers, such as Deutsche Bank have also put their asset management arm up for review but are yet to sell.

Factor-based investing and ETFs will be the two fastest growing segments in asset management.

Factor-based investing
Factor-based investing is a cool way to invest. A gentleman by the name of Andrew Ang is a pioneer in this space and has written a great book called Asset Management: A Systematic Approach to Factor Investing. It's investing based on a level more granular than the standard asset class (for example, equity investing, or alternatives investing). It's also one of the fastest growing areas in asset management with forecast annual organic growth rate of around 10%. 10% is very high. To put that into context, some of the traditional asset classes such as equities and fixed income are only expected to return low single digit annual organic growth. 1% or 2% is what I am referring to.

Recall the key asset classes. They include equities, fixed income, multi-assets, alternatives and cash. Factor-based investing is one level deeper. It's investing based on the fundamentals that drive these asset classes. There's a law in asset management, and indeed all of finance, called the mean-variance concept. The more common way it is referred to is risk and return, which we have touched upon earlier. Generally, the more risk you take, the more return you expect. Otherwise why would you take more risk if you didn't expect more return? Well it turns out there are a set of ingredients that drive risk and return in each asset class. Factor based investing is investing based on those underlying factors. It is a more targeted approach to investing. If asset classes are an elegant skyscraper then think of factors as the cement, steel, glass and other material required to create the building. If the cement is weak, and pulling down returns in your portfolio, then why not focus on investing in the glass and steel that look to be holding up well? Get the point?

A way of investing in this theme is to construct an index with similar securities. You can have lots of themes: a stock index full of stocks that exhibit low volatility, or an index of undervalued stocks that are underpriced. Or even stocks that seem to be performing well in current market conditions, called momentum stocks. There are lots of other themes but we won't go into too much detail.

The rise of factor-based investing comes down to one simple fact: it's harder to get good returns in volatile markets. There must be a way to be more selective in what you choose so that you can hone in on good returns. Smart Beta ETFs are an effective way to invest in factors. They enable investors to access broad factors categories in one go without having to worry about assembling the portfolio yourself.

ETFs: our much-loved index funds
ETFs... Who doesn't love ETFs? Good old ETFs. A great way to diversify your portfolio and an easy way to get broad exposure to any market you want. ETFs make up around $3 trillion in assets at the time of writing and is expected to double to $7 trillion after 2020 by consultant PwC. The reason why there will be so much growth is because ETFs are malleable and can be used for a variety of purposes. They actually play a prominent role in many of the leading trends such as the rising popularity of the retail channel, demand for factors based portfolios and demand for technology solutions in asset management. For example, many of the robo-advisors use ETFs to construct the optimal portfolio for investors. ETFs are simply great as building blocks for a variety of purposes.

As long as there is volatility in the markets, I predict

ETFs will continue to have a role. A portion of investors will fly to low-cost solutions because they just will not believe that active managers will be able to give them the sort of returns they are being paid for. ETFs will be one of the solutions. ETFs are expected to grow organically at over 10%, on par with factor-based investing.

Fee compression is real and will continue to take shape.

Why should I pay more for actively managed product when passive products have better long-term returns? Where's the value add? That's the question many are asking. Traditionally passive products have charged less than actively managed products because passive products only try to match the returns in the market while actively managed products try to beat the market and require skill to do so. There's regulation out there which is forcing asset management to be more transparent with the fee structure. This, coupled with the rising popularity of passive investing is forcing fees lower. Some predict fees might drop to zero for some products so that asset managers can first get the client on-board and then introduce them to more expensive actively-managed solutions. How convenient?

We are currently seeing around 1%-2% fee compression year-on-year across the industry. The average charge across the industry is around 40-50 basis points at the moment. A basis points is essentially a hundredth of a percentage. So 40-50 basis points means 0.4%-0.5%.

Closing remark on this chapter.

As you can see from this chapter, a lot of trends are closely intertwined. The impact is two-way for many trends. This is true of life in general. We live in a complex adaptive system where one factor impacts another and vice versa. Things then adapt based on how these various trends play out.

CHAPTER 6.
LEARNING THE LANGUAGE
THAT YOUR BOSS SPEAKS

Here are the key terms your boss is talking about in that important meeting.

If you really want to get under the skin of how people think and speak in the asset management world then you have to master the language. As ever, there is much confusion as to what the metrics actually mean. Let's go through the main ones and how they appear in your boss' conversations with their manager.

Assets under management (AUM)
AUM is short for assets under management. It is not the same as how much money the asset manager is generating. If you collect all the money your clients have given to you in trust to manage then that is what you call AUM. This is the key metric that gets thrashed out when comparing one asset manager to another. BlackRock, the world's largest asset manager has an astronomical $5T worth of money under management on behalf of their clients. The smallest manager may only have a

couple millions worth of assets. The problem with using AUM as the key metric with which to compare managers is that it can be entirely misleading. What about how much profit each manager is generating? AUM only tells you about how much money is being managed, it doesn't tell you how much profit is being generated by the manager or what they are charging for their services.

Fees

Enter fees: fees are usually referred to in basis point terms (100 basis points is the same as 1% fee). They are the middle ground between translating how much assets you have under management and how much revenue you are generating. Broadly, there is a formula that can solve this.

AUM x fees (in basis points) = revenue.

Simple but effective. You can already get a sense of how much money each manager is generating by studying their book of business and what the asset class mix is. Passive managers (those who offer funds that are only trying to track the market) will charge less than active managers (those who are continuously shuffling around their portfolios in order to try and beat the general market performance). In addition, those managers offering either equities, alternatives or multi-asset funds will generally be charging more than those managers offering cash or fixed income solutions because there is more volatility (risk) involved with managing equities, alternatives or multi-asset funds.

Revenue

Once you've compared AUM and fee rates, you'll have a sense of the company's revenue, and this my friend, is where I believe companies should be comparing each other. The problem with revenues is that not every company wants to reveal how much they are generating. The publicly listed managers have to reveal the numbers as part of their regular reporting duties, but for managers that are not yet listed on a stock exchange, there is no real requirement to reveal this. If you do observe the data out there you'll be astonished as to just how much variation there can be between managers. For example, Blackstone, a legendary asset manager in the alternatives space only has around $400 billion in assets under management at the time of writing but they generate around $11 billion in revenues annually. Compare this with Blackrock who manage $5 trillion (that's more than 10x the amount of Blackstone's assets) but generate $11 billion too. This is exactly the reason why AUM isn't the best metric available to compare asset managers. The two companies are entirely different animals and work in different ways. Both highly successful but both different to each other.

Organic asset growth
Next up is organic asset growth. This metric is extremely important to CEOs. Organic growth gives you an idea as to how much an asset manager grew by pulling in new business. In simple language, this is new flows as a percentage of starting assets. For example, if an asset manager had $100 billion in assets under management at the beginning of the year, and it gathered $7 billion in new assets from clients over the course of the year, then the organic growth is $7/$100 = 7%. 7% is considered high growth in the world of asset management. Anything over 10% is considered extremely fast and there's really only a few areas with that level of growth, ETFs for example.

Organic growth is an interesting metric because it enables you to move away from comparing absolute values (firm X gathered $11 billion, firm Y gathered $10 billion) and instead focus on context. If manager X has an asset base of $3 trillion and only managed to garner $11 billion, that would be considered far less successful than manager Y who only has $30 billion in assets under management but managed to pull in $10 billion. There's the context for you!

Another piece of insight is that as the asset base grows, it becomes harder to continue growing at a fast pace because diminishing returns kicks in. You'll therefore find some of the larger asset categories, such as active fixed income, growing at a slower pace than niche areas, such as factors investing. This is a basic law of nature but just as applicable in asset management as it is elsewhere.

Inorganic growth

Inorganic growth is the opposite of organic growth. It's usually what CEOs prefer not to focus on, but in reality they frequently do. Inorganic growth is when you get a boost in assets due to an acquisition of another manager. The assets of the two firms combine to create a larger firm. Many companies tend to omit inorganic growth when focusing on the performance of the company because it's not really business that you generated. It's more so a one-off boost in assets. Equally, if you are comparing your asset growth to the general industry, management may be compelled to include in inorganic growth in order to reflect 'rapid asset growth'.

Compounded annual growth rate (CAGR)

CAGR stands for compounded annual growth rate and reflects the year-on-year growth of assets from point A to point B in time. More accurately, it can be described as follows:

CAGR = starting AUM + organic growth + inorganic growth + market performance (beta) + FX movements = new AUM

Notice how the formula includes organic growth. That is absolutely valid. CAGR describes everything that can take assets from A to B. That will be a mix of how much new assets the manager won during the period (organic growth), the general growth in the value of assets in the market (market performance) and any currency effects that can change the value of assets when converting from Euros to US Dollars, for example.

From a mathematical sense, think of CAGR as the line of best fit that you can insert through a wave. The wave is the trajectory of assets from point A to B, which would describe a period of a number of years. CAGR describes the rate it would take to achieve today's assets if you grew at a steady constant rate from point A.

CLOSING REMARKS

And there we have it. A primer on the industry. Not on portfolio management. We have covered many topics in this short introduction. Everything from who the main industry players are, who the main client types are, to understanding some of the lingo used by people in the business day-to-day. You now have a big picture view of the industry.

Printed in Great Britain
by Amazon